Conte

GW00363452

The Savill Garden
Wick Lane
Englefield Green
Surrey
TW20 0UU

www.theroyallandscape.co.uk

Foreword

The Crown Estate has a unique and diverse property portfolio encompassing commercial, residential, marine and rural holdings throughout the country. As a business it has two main objectives: to benefit the taxpayer by paying the revenue from its assets directly to the Exchequer, and to enhance the value of the estate and the income it generates. The Crown Estate includes amongst its diverse portfolio many historically important buildings and environmentally sensitive landscapes, and the core values which guide its management are commercialism, integrity and stewardship.

Windsor Great Park is the only Royal Park owned by The Crown Estate. The Royal Landscape, an area of some 1,000 acres in the south-east corner of the Park encompassing The Savill and Valley Gardens and Virginia Water, is without question a national asset and requires our careful management and stewardship.

We receive hundreds of thousands of visitors from home and abroad every year and we have an obligation not only to ensure people enjoy their experience, but that the landscape is conserved, and improved, for future generations.

The Savill Building has been designed as a major step in the programme to improve the management of The Royal Landscape and the investment in it. The dramatic design, with its distinctive swooping roof, has provided us with a landmark building: a gateway to the garden itself, as well as to Valley Gardens and Virginia Water.

The development of the building has evolved over a period of five years and the team dedicated to this work have looked at every detail of the building and its surroundings. It is a tribute to all concerned that the end product is such an exciting and challenging building which nevertheless provides all the facilities required by our visitors.

Philip Everett, Deputy Ranger of Windsor Great Park
The Crown Estate

Introduction

When The Crown Estate was seeking an architect for its new building at The Savill Garden, it was keen that the finished design should be innovative and iconic but buildable, that it should enhance the image of the gardens while being sustainable. Glenn Howells Architects' building managed to meld these sometimes conflicting requirements into a fine new structure, heralding a new era for the gardens.

The elegant curved roof sits comfortably in the landscape. The form of the gridshell structure mimics the hills and valleys of the surrounding Windsor Great Park. The main materials of this innovative structure were harvested within the surrounding area, a testament to the ingenuity of the design.

The new building greatly enhances the amenities on the site – the shop, garden centre and restaurant – and presents a new face to the outside world. It will help raise the profile of the gardens and attract new audiences who may be unaware of the botanical treasures they contain.

Over the past decade, Glenn Howells Architects have built a strong reputation for well thought-out buildings and quality architecture, with designs that are specific to the particular site and requirement. At The Savill Garden they have produced an exciting building that will become a defining image of The Royal Landscape.

The Royal Landscape
within Windsor Great Park

This ambitious landscaping and plantation project began in the late 17th century, initially inspired by the formal gardens of the French landscape architect, André le Nôtre, whom Charles II encountered when in exile. This admiration for continental garden design was shared by William III and Mary, and their gardener, Henry Wise, who also worked for Queen Anne, created terraces, avenues and other formal features within the landscape. It was, however, George II's younger son, William Augustus, Duke of Cumberland, who transformed the landscape when he became Ranger in 1746, putting into practice much of what he'd learned about classical architecture from architect Henry Flitcroft, another architect, John Vardy, and topographical draughtsman Thomas Sandby.

The area of The Royal Landscape covers a thousand acres of gardens, lakes and woodland in the south-east corner of Windsor Great Park. This is a fifth of the total area of the park, which stretches from Windsor Castle in the north to Ascot in the south. Hundreds of thousands of people – from local residents to overseas visitors – enjoy the tranquility and splendour of the largest and oldest open space in the densely-populated south-east of England.

Many visitors are unaware of the gardens at the heart of The Royal Landscape: The Savill Garden and The Valley Gardens on the banks of Virginia Water. That will change, thanks to the restoration project currently underway, and thanks to improved visitor facilities, spearheaded by the arresting new Savill Building.

The Royal Landscape lies in the counties of Surrey and Berkshire. The park has royal connections that date back to Edward the Confessor (who reigned from 1042-1066). The origins of the park are closely associated with the fortified Saxon town at Old Windsor, in Berkshire, used as a royal residence both before and after the Norman invasion. The land to the south-west of Old Windsor was ideal hunting territory, comprising both heathland and forest. It was enclosed in the 13th century to provide an extensive area for hunting deer and wild boar.

The park was extended in around 1313 when Edward II added a further 146 acres to the north-west. An exact date has not been determined for when the Great Park spread beyond the Berkshire boundary into Surrey, although documents exist to show that the park contained some Surrey land by the early 14th century. In 1359, in Edward III's reign, a further notable addition was made with the acquisition, enclosure and extension of the manor of Wychemere, and surrounding arable land, to the north-east of the old park. It was within the parish of Old Windsor and covered a large area from the site of the moated manor to the Berkshire-Surrey border to the south.

By the end of the 14th century the various enclosures to the south of Windsor were combined into a single unit known as the Great Park, and Wychemere demolished. The Great Park was now distinct and separate from the Little Park which had been attached to the castle since 1368. In the 16th century the royal forests and woods were seriously depleted owing to the demands made on them by the navy, and there were many new plantations.

In 1680 Charles II planted the majestic elm tree avenue, known as The Long Walk, linking Windsor Castle with the Great Park. This was the catalyst for an active period of landscaping and building. Lodges were built during the 17th and 18th centuries to house the park administrators, one of whom, William Augustus, Duke of Cumberland, oversaw the flooding of Virginia Water lake.

Cumberland also introduced to Windsor the new fashion for garden design, as first seen in the work of both Lord Burlington and William Kent two decades earlier. His emphasis was in line with contemporary ideas of a more natural, picturesque landscape adorned with ornate bridges, cascades, grottos – even a Mandarin Yacht and an oriental building on China Island.

Thomas Sandby continued to work under George III, restoring Virginia Water after its destruction by flood in 1768. John Robinson, the Surveyor General of Woods and Forests, transformed the north shore of the lake, what is now the Valley Gardens, turning the scrubby heathland into a mixed woodland landscape.

The Georgian period is perhaps most obviously marked by the equestrian statue of the King, known as the Copper Horse, at the southern end of The Long Walk.

The farms and forests within the park were further developed during Queen Victoria's reign, when her husband, Prince Albert, was Ranger of the Park. Much of the tree planting is a legacy of the Victorian era, as are the estate workers' cottages, and the Royal School, which still educates pupils today. During the 20th century this concern for the workers and their families was further advanced with the establishment of a village, including a social club and a local shop.

In landscaping terms, the highlight of the last century was the creation in the 1930s and 1940s of The Savill Garden and The Valley Gardens. In the Second World War, the deer lawns and pasture were converted to arable stock to help the war effort. The deer herds remained absent from the park until 1979, when as Ranger HRH The Duke of Edinburgh reintroduced them.

The variety within the park, from ancient ruins and Georgian houses to statues, monuments, fortresses and farms, is the work of many landscape architects and gardeners. The current horticultural and building project aims both to protect and to further the heritage of The Royal Landscape, enlarging and enhancing the gardens and restoring some of the Georgian landscape features. As Keeper of the Gardens Mark Flanagan explains, 'by bringing the elements together – The Savill Garden, The Valley Gardens and the landscape of Virginia Water – we are renewing the spirit that animated the great landscape architects and horticulturists of previous centuries.'

The gardens of The Royal Landscape

The creation of landscaped gardens under the direction of Sir Eric Savill, with the encouragement of King George V and the Duke of York (later King George VI), brought about the most significant change to the southern area of Windsor Great Park.

The Savill Garden

In 1931, when Sir Eric Savill was appointed Deputy Surveyor at Windsor, there was no garden within Windsor Great Park. Savill's knowledge of horticulture secured him royal approval for a gardening project, and by 1934 he was showing King George V and Queen Mary around what was initially called the Bog Garden. Over the next five years he was able to extend the area to the west and south to its present size of 35 acres. Savill was made Deputy Ranger of the park in 1937. By decree of George VI the garden was renamed after its creator in July 1951.

The Savill Garden's purpose is purely to delight. It is, as Keeper of the Gardens Mark Flanagan says, 'a place of enchantment', created out of what on first consideration must have seemed an unlikely site in the south-east corner of the estate. A tangle of brambles and bracken with impenetrable thickets of rhododendron ponticum sprawled over the undulating site, which had a mixture of poor, free draining Bagshot sand and wet, cloying peat. Despite the apparent adversity of the location, Savill's selection proved wise. The mature forest trees of oak, beech and sweet chestnut, originally planted in the 18th century by the Duke of Cumberland, provided an excellent framework for Savill's vision of a woodland garden. The diverse soil meant that a wide range of plants could be cultivated, and the presence of a small stream, which trickled towards Obelisk Pond, was another useful resource.

Work to realise Savill's dream began in the winter of 1932, with the clearing away of many of the thickets in the north-west corner of the garden, close to where the Queen Elizabeth Temperate House stands today. Brightly coloured flowering plants from East Asia and North America, including rhododendrons and azaleas, magnolia and camellias were cultivated, with irises and primulas in the wetter ground surrounding the ponds.

As visitor numbers increased, the decision was taken to expand the Spring theme within the woodlands and to concentrate on introducing new features within the garden. This included the rose gardens, which were added in the 1950s, along with a double herbaceous border, raised beds and wall plantings. By the mid 1950s, the structure of the garden was very much as it can be seen today.

Sir Eric Savill directed work on the garden until he retired in 1970. His vision was continued by Thomas Hope Findlay, Keeper of the The Savill Garden, who retired in 1975, and new features were added by his successor, John Bond. This included, in 1978, the Jubilee Garden, a predominantly autumnal display of colour, and the innovative Dry Garden (an inspiration from the droughts of the late 1970s). The Queen Elizabeth Temperate House was opened in 1995 and the latest major addition was the Golden Jubilee Garden, opened in 2002, a modern interpretation of a cottage garden with a water sculpture by Barry Mason at its centre.

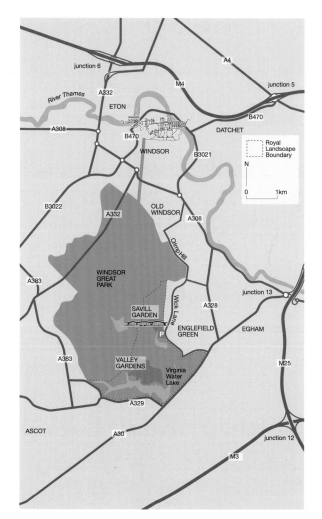

Below: The gardens of The Royal Landscape comprise a wide range of planting, from forest to herbaceous borders.

Today, Harvey Stephens is the Head of The Savill Garden, overseen by Mark Flanagan. Mark has travelled widely, including visits to South Korea, Taiwan and mainland China, collecting seeds of plants to complement the garden's native species, thereby ensuring the garden's continuing diversity.

The Valley Gardens

The Savill Garden is regarded as 'the elder sibling' of The Valley Gardens, explains Mark Flanagan. In 1946 estate staff were returning from service during the Second World War and Sir Eric Savill and his team were keen to continue horticultural development within the park. Savill had run out of room for expansion on his original site, but he still had plenty of ambition. After selecting a patch of ground on the north shores of the 18th century man-made Virginia Water, with its undulating valleys and mature broadleaved trees providing a canopy of dappled shade, work began on realising Savill's next great gardening project.

At 35 acres The Savill Garden is considerably smaller than the 200-acre Valley Gardens, but due to its accessibility, in contrast to the lengthy woodland walk required to reach The Valley Gardens, the elder of the two gardens has tended to attract more visitors. The ambition of The Royal Landscape project is to bring some coherence to The Savill and Valley Gardens, and Virginia Water. The new Savill Building will act as a portal to all three.

In landscaping The Valley Gardens, Savill understood the role that Virginia Water could play in providing an eye-catching vista at the end of the valleys. The valleys were steep-sided on the western side, becoming shallower as they progressed east to be lost in the great forest plantations. He also realised, says Flanagan, 'the strength of the framework provided by the parallel valleys in setting the structure for the proposed plantings.'

Five sweeping valleys make up The Valley Gardens, the most famous of which is the Punch Bowl, which is filled with an abundance of multicoloured azaleas. Sir Eric Savill and Hope Findlay determined that this new garden should be conceived as a large scale woodland garden with expansive plantings. 'The central design thesis', explains Flanagan, 'was to create a flowering forest, a natural woodland in which the overall impression was of a scene in some far part of China or the uplands of the Appalachian mountains in eastern North America.'

Key groups of plants include rhododendrons, azaleas and camellias, with flowering cherries, magnolias, exotic oaks, sweet gums, tupelos, Asiatic rowans, the handkerchief tree and countless maples added to the canopy. Beneath the canopy the rhododendrons are joined by plants such as witch-hazels and flowering dogwoods, and the woodland floor is covered by hostas, ferns and other associated plants.

National Collections at Windsor

Plants are not immune to the vagaries of fashion, and as a result species can sometimes die out if the demand for them fades away. In 1978 the Royal Horticultural Society set up an initiative that eventually led to the formation of the National Council for the Conservation of Plants and Gardens (NCCPG), a nationwide association of individuals who work together to prevent garden plants from becoming extinct. The NCCPG set up a National Collections scheme to conserve garden plants, registering collections and encouraging and helping their owners to grow as wide a range of their chosen plant group as possible. In The Savill Garden and The Valley Gardens there are eight such groups designated as National Collections, one of the largest numbers on a single site, forming an integral part of the gardens. They are magnolia, mahonia, pernettya, rhododendron species, rhododendron Glenn Dale azaleas, hardy ferns, ilex and dwarf conifers.

The Savill Building

The dramatic, undulating roof of The Savill Building has already become the identifiable icon of The Royal Landscape. It has been compared variously to a spaceship, a leaf and an upturned boat. Whatever visitors' perceptions, it is clear that the building, particularly its roof, has captured the imagination and drawn public attention to The Savill Garden and The Royal Landscape.

In 1963, the first visitor centre for The Savill Garden was built to provide visitors to the garden with the opportunity for refreshment, an apparently essential component for a complete day out (as evidenced by the immediate doubling of visitor numbers). In 1976 a modest conservatory structure followed, doubling as a giftshop and a plant sales facility. By 1986 a more substantial stone-clad shop was added. Over four decades later the original visitor centre was seriously outdated.

The architectural competition

The brief to the architects was for an environmentally sensitive building that would nevertheless leave a dramatic mark on the landscape. To encourage more innovative ideas, it was decided to consider younger, lesser known architects and a shortlist of three was drawn up, all of whom offered contemporary ideas that marked a departure from The Crown Estate's past commissions.

The submission from Glenn Howells Architects proposed a pioneering method of constructing the roof which had only been used once before on a project by Edward Cullinan Architects at the Weald and Downland Open Air Museum in Singleton. Here, the architects, along with consulting engineers Buro Happold, had constructed an award-winning double layer timber gridshell as a workshop and storage area for the museum, known as the Downland Gridshell.

The design brief was to combine the best of modern engineering with traditional craft skills. It was felt that this was what was needed at The Savill Garden.

The Savill Building project team visited the Downland Gridshell to see the impressive building first hand. What they saw, says Mark Flanagan, Keeper of the Gardens, 'knocked us out'.

Innovative timber construction

The visit gave the client confidence in Howells' project. 'We knew we could have an exciting building', says Philip Everett. 'This concept fulfilled the brief that we should have a statement building – something that people would talk about and that would last.'

Although both buildings have significant ancillary rooms they are essentially single cell spaces, oversailed by a gridshell roof. While the Downland building is much smaller – and different in many respects to Howells' concept – it provided a graphic illustration of what could be achieved using innovative new techniques in greenwood timber construction. What was more, it soon became apparent that the expansive roof could be constructed using the Estate's own timber.

One of The Crown Estate's key concerns when selecting the architect was that the new building should sit comfortably and unobtrusively within the Park. It was felt that the landscape received this building better than the others. There was no doubt that while this would be an iconic piece of architecture, it would be subtle and respectful of the landscape it aimed to support and promote.

Creative collaboration

The Savill Building houses a shop, restaurant and visitor centre. It is 90 metres long, up to 25 metres wide and 4.5 to 8.5 metres high. May 2004 saw the inauguration of the £5.35 million project, with site work beginning in October that year.

A year later, on 9 May 2005, Deputy Ranger Philip Everett started the 'bending' of the roof timbers; the ceremonial launch of a process that shaped the structure into its distinctive double-curve.

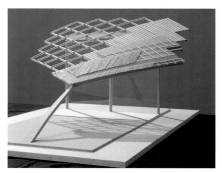
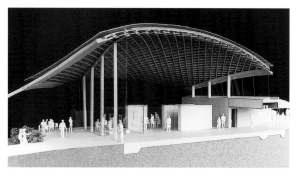

Below: Schoolchildren bury a time capsule on site in June 2004 at the same time as the larch for the roof is sourced. Photographs show the selection, felling, collection and preparation of the larch.
Opposite: Beams being positioned.

Opposite: The building under construction viewed from The Savill Garden
Below: Angie Mullen, The Crown Estate; Laurie Braden, Inwood; Graham Gamblin, Michael Curran, Steve Corbett, Damien Rose, Chris Doody, Daniel Sargent, Andrew Holloway, William Flynn, Darren Cocking, Edward Rice, Green Oak Carpentry Company; Nigel Braden, Inwood; Stephen Haskins, Haskins Robinson Waters; Andrew Rapmund, Back Group; Jamie Webb, Glenn Howells Architects; Mark Flanagan, The Crown Estate; Phil Roberts, Ridge; Philip Everett, Jan Bartholomew, Andrew Dunning, The Crown Estate; Richard Austin, Clinton Church, Jim Houliman, Phoenix; Mark Bunton, Graham Hilton, Byron Hanston, Michael Segbafah, Verry.

The realisation of the architect's concept has been a truly collaborative effort. 'It was our choice to work bottom up, from the start', explains Howells. 'Our ideas were only ever going to be as good as the advice we got from our sub-contractors, particularly when it came to the roof. We designed around what was possible, testing each idea with the carpenters, structural engineers for the roof and the client.'

Although the broad concept for the building remained unchanged, the aesthetic details followed on from this exploration of structure and materials. The organic, undulating form came about because of how the building would perform – structurally, environmentally and spatially – rather than simply how it would look; in the same way that a leaf looks the way it does because of its function, rather than because it looks nice.

In keeping with the intention that the building should meld into the landscape, the exterior is architecturally more subdued than the interior. On entering the heart of the building, one experiences a sense of wonder similar to arriving inside a great cathedral. The eyes are automatically drawn upwards and, scanning the length of the building, thoughts turn to the skill of the engineers and craftsmen. How have they achieved this feat? The rippling timber, as seemingly pliable as a magic carpet, appears to be held aloft by supernatural powers. It simultaneously promotes feelings of lightness, a result of its structure, and reassuring permanence, as suggested by the solidity of the timber.

What is a gridshell?

The term 'gridshell' is derived from the naturally strong structure of the sea shell. A gridshell – which can be constructed of timber, steel or concrete – is a shell with holes, but with the structure concentrated into strips. Once built, timber gridshells are immensely strong structures. While under construction the individual timber elements are remarkably pliable, behaving almost like stiff rubber. This allows for the material to be deformed into a shape and then locked.

The Savill gridshell is in four layers, with a regular one metre grid of 80 x 50mm larch. The three-domed shape is clad in oak and has a tubular steel beam running around the perimeter, held in place by steel quadruped legs. Before the consultants could set about realising the gridshell, the timber was sourced from The Crown Estate's woodland within the Windsor Estate. Derick Stickler, Chief Forester of the Windsor Estate, Tom Compton of English Woodlands Timber, who processed the timber, and Green Oak Carpentry walked the commercially managed woodland in Windsor forest to discuss what was needed and examine where it might come from. The trees were selectively felled and graded by the Windsor estate's forestry department, leaving six to eight trees per hectare to grow in perpetuity as the ecological resource. The success of the roof shows what can be achieved with home grown timber, when trees are managed with care.'

A full-scale roof section was built as a prototype to refine the structural details. The timber was cut using a high-tech sawmill, which cuts the maximum amount with the least wastage. Once this was done, the 'finger-jointing' began. The defects in the wood, such as knots, were marked up and cut out. The timber was then rejoined using polyurethane adhesive and finger-joints. These joints, which are only visible close up, are used to achieve 'improved timber', graded to the specific structural requirement for its performance.

At the end of cutting and joining process the team were left with 10,000 metres of best quality larch, and a further 10,000 metres of low-grade timber, cut into 6 metre lengths for transportation. In total, just over 20 kilometres of timber were used, roughly the equivalent of the distance between Windsor Castle and Hampton Court Palace, and it weighs 30 tonnes. This is considerably less than the weight of an equivalent steel roof. Gridshell structures are comparatively lightweight, while being structurally and environmentally efficient.

The six metre lengths of timber were delivered to site where they were extended to 36 metre lengths using 'scarf jointing'. These lengths of timber took eight men to carry onto the roof, where they were laid onto the flat lattice on a scaffold grid and connected together.

Above the gridshell structure is an aluminium roof system, with 160mm of insulation and a profiled standing-seam skin. It serves as the waterproof layer and support for the oak rain-screen. Oak cladding was chosen, not only for its impressive resilience, but because it will weather to a silvery grey and the original concept was to see the curve of the building's roof representing the top of the tree line.

Opposite: The roof building team sit on the structure just before it is covered in ply.

Below: Photographs show the distinctive form of the gridshell taking shape and the final stages of completing the roof.

Beyond the roof

The gridshell is supported by an earth structure on the entrance elevation, housing ancillary service spaces including the kitchen, storerooms and washrooms, concealed by a earth 'roof' designed and planted with juniper by the horticultural staff of The Savill Garden. On the garden elevation the terrace is slightly raised and fully enclosed, with a curved glazed curtain wall providing spectacular views across the landscape. An independent glazing system was required due to the inevitable movement of the timbers in the roof.

To enhance the views into the garden through the glazed wall, the gardens team designed three vistas from the building in the shape of a trident, the central vista acting as the entrance walk into the garden. The oak is very much a signature tree at Windsor, with its large population of veteran oaks. Not only does the building have an oak roof and floor, but also the avenue leading into the garden is lined with upright oaks, with mature oaks all around it.

Glenn Howells Architects initially considered a rammed-earth wall or dry stone for the front and the return and flank walls, but ultimately chose brickwork which provides colour variation and an almost hand-thrown, garden-wall aesthetic.

Howells was keen that the material used should relate to the existing garden walls, further ensuring that the building complements and introduces the landscape, rather than competing with it.

Russ Canning & Company Limited worked on the restoration elements of the landscape architecture in The Royal Landscape project. The company's involvement with the building included developing an entrance walkway into the garden itself. The avenue of trees draws visitors through the building and provides an additional means of orientation. The new landscaping makes the parking area a part of the visiting experience. A decision was taken to plant only native species in the car park, with nothing exotic to distract from the axial design.

'From the car park approach, the building should appear as part of the rhododendron perimeter, thus playing down the back of house accommodation and allowing the project to read as simply timber roof and landscape', explains Howells.

Inside the building

Inside, the floor also showcases oak from The Crown Estate. The floor, complete with underfloor heating, was laid by Weldon Flooring.

The key elements of the interior are two white corian 'pods' that define the interior functions without diminishing the effect of the vaulted roof. The team also worked closely with Avid, the designers of the restaurant and shop, in order to establish a consistent language between all aspects of the project.

At the entrance to the building, beneath the paving, lies a time capsule which was prepared and filled by the pupils of the Royal School, located in Windsor Great Park. It was buried in 2004. We hope that it is many decades, if not centuries, before the building's useful life expires and the capsule is unearthed.

The Royal opening

The Savill Building was officially opened in June 2006 by HRH The Duke of Edinburgh who is Ranger of Windsor Great Park. For this special occasion His Royal Highness unveiled a commemorative plaque at the entrance to The Savill Building, on Queen's Avenue, and was then taken on a tour of the building and around the terrace into The Savill Garden. He also met children from the Royal School and was shown where their time capsule was buried.

From the first day of opening, the building has earned enthusiastic reviews for its stunning architecture, both from local users of Windsor Great Park and visitors and press from further afield. The Savill Building has become a popular venue for both shopping and eating. Visitors can stroll out under the canopy of the roof, with ample natural light shining through the west-facing glass wall.

The Wood Awards

Within a few months of its opening, The Savill Building had already earned its architectural laurels, winning Gold at the prestigious Wood Awards. The Wood Awards recognise, encourage and promote outstanding design and craftsmanship. In addition, it also won awards in the categories of 'Commercial and Public Access' and 'Structural', beating off stiff competition from buildings such as the National Assembly for Wales. This is the first time in 30 years one building has won the three awards in the same year. The judges were unanimous in their praise for the building: 'The beautiful magic of the building is exposed to visitors very slowly. Internally, the effect is one of light and space; it is a very pleasant place to be.'

Civic Trust Awards

The building also won a Civic Trust Award Special Award. The citation described it as a 'beautiful new visitor centre which combines the technological and the natural. The undulating timber gridshell roof is very attractive from both within and outside the building. Car parking to the front of the building is well considered and gives an interesting view of the roof.'

Looking ahead

Chief Executive of The Crown Estate, Roger Bright is confident that The Savill Building will provide 'a magnificent new entrance' to the Garden, and The Royal Landscape as a whole. He sees the beautifully designed and thoughtfully planned building as emblematic of the wider ambitions of The Royal Landscape project, which seeks to improve the management of, and investment in, The Savill Garden, Valley Gardens, Virginia Water and the land that links them, as is consistent with The Crown Estate's values and ambitions for the entire Windsor estate.

As well as this major new building there are proposals (still subject to planning) for a smaller visitor facility adjacent to Virginia Water, as well as improvements to the adjoining car park. The landscape restoration programme, which includes extensive tree planting and the recovery of lost 18th century vistas, is to be carried out in accordance with recommendations made by Russ Canning Landscape Architects, and supported by English Nature, English Heritage and other statutory bodies. Repairs to the Leptis Magna ruins and the Virginia Water Cascade will also be implemented over a five year period.

The wider landscape

In 2007 The Savill Garden celebrates its 75th anniversary and to mark the occasion the New Zealand Garden was opened in April by HRH The Duke of York KG KCVO. This new attraction houses nearly 3,000 of New Zealand's native plants, gathered together for the first time in the UK in a ground-breaking initiative.

The New Zealand Garden began as a gift to HM The Queen following a state visit in 1986.

The relocation of the visitor facilities to The Savill Building has allowed for the development of a more ambitious New Zealand Garden with the addition of many new specimens.

Now the building is in full operation it serves as the gateway to The Royal Landscape. The plans for improved facilities at Valley Gardens and Virginia Water will only enhance the visitor experience across the whole of The Royal Landscape.

Designed and produced by Wordsearch, 85 Clerkenwell Road, London EC1R 5AR. Photography by Warwick Sweeney. Text by Nicola Jackson. Additional text by JDD Consulting. Images on pages 5 and 6 courtesy of The Royal Collection © 2006 HM Queen Elizabeth II